PROCESS AND MINISTRY

Bruce G. Epperly

Topical Line Drives
Volume 30

Energion Publications
Gonzalez, Florida
2018

Electronic Editions:
Adobe Digital Editions: 978-1-63199-551-4
Kindle: 978-1-63199-552-1
iBooks: 978-1-63199-553-8
Google Play: 978-1-63199-554-5
Aer.io: 978-1-63199-555-2

ISBN10: 1-63199-541-3
ISBN13: 978-1-63199-541-5

Energion Publications
P. O. Box 841
Gonzalez, FL 32560

pubs@energion.com
energion.com

TABLE OF CONTENTS

A WORD OF INVITATION
FROM CLAREMONT TO CAPE COD
AND BACK AGAIN

Recently, I had a dream. I was a given spacious study, perhaps forty by twenty feet, in the basement of an academic building at a major seminary. My study had no walls and people came in and out as I sat reading in my professorial wing chair. Some stopped briefly to chat, while others simply passed through on their way to other destinations. A few even lingered for theological conversations The dream concluded with a voice affirming, "You are surely blessed to have a study without walls."

A study without walls! Perhaps, the comment was autobiographical. For over thirty-five years, I have joined classroom and pulpit, contemplation and action, and theological reflection and ministerial practice. I have routinely crossed boundaries, separating pastoral ministry from academic life and Christian faith and the world of spiritual diversity. I have consciously sought to be both "spiritual and religious," committed institutionally to the church and my vocation as pastor while embracing wisdom from a variety of spiritual experiences, including the insights of persons from other faiths. My faith has grown "on the boundary," to quote Paul Tillich, where bridges have replaced walls and margins have become frontiers.

A study without walls! A church without walls! Academic life immersed in the messiness of postmodern pilgrimages. A church whose boundaries are permeable and practices flexible. A church that welcomes seekers, sharing and receiving wisdom in the process. A ministerial life that is open-spirited, dynamic, and hopeful. Pastoral leadership that discovers unexpected possibilities in the concrete limitations of twenty-first century congregational life. Ministry without walls or fences!

This text had its origins in 2012 when I was asked to be Visiting Professor of Process Studies at Claremont School of Theology in Claremont, California. In the heart of process theology, I taught a seminar of "Process and Ministry" to a lively group of seminarians, graduate students, and working pastors. Fast forward five years, I was again asked to teach a course on "Process Theology, Spirituality, and Ministry," this time through the wanders of cyber technology that gathered students from across the country for on-line seminars and digital dialogues. During this five year interval, I left full-time seminary teaching and administration to pastor an historic village church on Cape Cod, Massachusetts.

Living professionally without walls as a scholar, teacher, and pastor, I have for the past five years brought my academic insights to congregational life. Congregational leadership has, conversely, shaped my academic perspective. As a working village pastor, I have daily experienced the challenges of growing a congregation spiritually, theologically, and numerically in an environment where institutional religion has been pushed to the sidelines. Every day, I encounter persons with deep spiritual yearnings who believe the church is the last place to find the spiritual nurture they long for. This text reflects my own emerging and tentative vision of pastoral ministry, based on the insights of process theology, as these relate to the challenges pastors face today.

In the interdependent world of cyber technology, most pastors can, with excitement or frustration, affirm John Wesley's maxim, my parish is the world. But, with fewer resources, vague guidelines for success, and uncertainty about the future of ministry and the church, the global nature of ministry is unsettling and overwhelming, to say the least. How can pastors follow the way of Jesus in our 24/7 world? How can we discover a life-affirming vision of ministry, whether we are full-time and overworked or part-time and trying to draw healthy boundaries?

As a process theologian, I believe the physical, geographical, and spiritual limitations we experience are the womb of possibilities. In the concreteness of life, we discover God's vision for ourselves and our congregations. This brief text seeks to provide a flexible and open-ended vision for 21st century ministry in our postmodern, pluralistic, and post-Christian world. I give thanks to those who have inspired my reflections, the students of my two Claremont seminars; the congregation and staff of South Congregational Church, Centerville, Massachusetts, and in particular my

1

colleague in ministry Pamela Wannie; my colleagues in the emerging church movement, Brian McLaren, Carol Howard Merritt, Doug Pagitt, and Diana Butler Bass; my academic and spiritual companions, Jay McDaniel, Patricia Adams Farmer, John Philip Newell, and Monica Coleman; my teachers, John Cobb, David Griffin, and Bernard Loomer; and my wife Kate and our Cape Cod family. I also want to thank members of my Claremont School of Theology "Process Theology, Spirituality and Ministry" class whose spiritual journeys inspired me to undertake this project. As always, thanks to my publisher at Energion, Henry Neufeld, for his creative synthesis of many voices for today's spiritual environment and Energion's editorial staff, Jody Neufeld and Chris Eyre.

As we embark on this spiritual voyage in process-relational ministry, I and many others feel like the Celtic spirit guides who launched out to see on small boats, coracles, rudderless and often not knowing where they were going, but charting their courses by the stars and trusting that God's gentle providence would lead them to their place of resurrection, the destination toward which grace and gift guide our paths. The way ahead is wide open for congregations and pastors, but when we share our commitments to God's unfolding vision we become part of a lively community where all are pilgrims but none are strangers.

CHAPTER ONE
IT'S ALL IN THE PROCESS

The story is told of the Greek philosopher Heraclitus, who claimed "you can't step in the same waters twice." An upstart pupil countered, "you can't even step in the same waters once. While you're dipping your foot in the river, the stream has already passed you, bringing new water to bathe your feet."

When I was young, the older generation used to describe slowly moving decision-making processes as traveling at glacial speed. Today, this comparison no longer applies. With the advance of global climate change, glaciers are collapsing at breakneck speed in some parts of the world, portending rising sea levels and threats to coastal cities. Whether by nature or human artifice, life is a process of change or as Alfred North Whitehead, the intellectual parent of process theology asserted, the process is the reality.

Process theology affirms the lively, ever-evolving, ever-changing nature of reality. Each moment of experience emerges from its immediate past and then gives birth in its own creativity to a novel, evolving future. Process and relationship characterize every living thing, from the smallest cell to the Soul of the Universe. Regardless of how we imagine the nature of theological reflection and the practice of ministry, we must understand them in terms of movement and relationship. Church and ministry must be agile and creative to match the novelty of our rapidly-changing cultural and planetary environment.

Process theology, or process-relational theology, seeks to join biblical spirituality with the insights of theology, science, literature, psychology, and philosophy. Not content with a compartmentalized or dualistic vision of reality, process theology describes the world in terms of holistic relationships, applicable to both creatures and their Creator. The Living God is faithful, yet God's mercies are new every morning. Nothing can separate us from the love of God, yet God is constantly doing a new thing. God's loving vision is changeless, yet God is still speaking. God's gentle providence interacts with all creation in a constant process of call and response

3

through which God shapes and is shaped by God's relationships with each creature and the creative process in its totality.

Process theologians believe that ministry is grounded in metaphysics. How we understand our world, at the micro and macro level, will shape our understanding of the calling of the church and our calling as pastors. If we see the world as divided into essentially unrelated units, we will see the church as well as the nation forging its vocation apart from culture and context. Congregational or national well-being will be an end in and of itself, focusing on church growth or America first as ultimate goals. In contrast, process theologians believe that if we see the world as interdependent, we will recognize that our congregation and nation depend on factors beyond ourselves and see our mission as bringing healing to the world in which we all matter to each another. Embedded yet with goals beyond our cultural context, church and pastor will engage in prophetic healing, honoring and yet critiquing the ambient culture and social context.

With no clear map or destination, process theology presents a lively vision, which serves as a polestar for creative congregational and ministerial practices. The basic affirmations of process-relational theology, relevant to life-changing ministry, include:

1) *Dynamic Interdependence.* We are all part of a lively and intricate web of relationships. Each moment emerges from the vastness of the universe and its immediate environment and contributes by its own creative process to the world beyond itself. Connected with one another in a dynamic universe, we shape each other's realities for good or ill. There are no self-made persons. The wealthy and powerful depend on the vulnerable and impoverished for their largesse, and the vulnerable are often at the mercy of impersonal and often uncaring powers and principalities that determine their fate. What happens to polar bears and plankton shapes human survival and human actions shape weather patterns that protect or destroy our non-human environment. In a dynamic, relational universe, ethics involves promoting authentic beauty and value

4

wherever it occurs, most especially among the least of these and those who suffer in body, mind, and spirit.

2) *Re-enchanting Reality.* The ancients saw reality as magical and spirit-filled. Beneath the physical world, they saw the movements of spiritual beings. Certain places were considered holy, "thin places," where heaven and earth interpenetrated each other and persons could travel from one dimension to another. In its desire for control, the modern world exorcised spirit from nature and ultimately humankind. The world became flat, matter in motion, explainable completely by the five senses, and existing solely to be manipulated by human artifice, without any consideration to ethics or value of the non-human world. In contrast, process theology affirms a reenchanted universe, full of energy and life, permeated by Spirit, and yet affirmative of science and technology. Process theology is grounded in a deeper empiricism in which experience is universal and not occasional. Non-human animals feel pain and joy, and deserve moral consideration. The heavens declare the glory of God and so do our intestines. As the Psalmist says, everything that breathes praises God. The world is alive, filled with energy and spirit, and revelatory of divine wisdom. Our ethical and spiritual calling is to nurture appreciation, affirmation, and amazement at the intricately connected and dynamic universe of experience and to promote value and beauty by our relationships to one another and the non-human world. Ethics demands that we save the baby whales as well as the baby humans, and honor the wonder of flora and fauna as our beloved companions.

3) *Holy Adventure.* A re-enchanted world gives birth to freedom and creativity. Each moment of experience, whether human or non-human, contributes something new to the universe. Grounded in divine creativity, the world is constantly being reborn. God's creativity is new every morning and invites us to be creators as well. Higher organisms, like ourselves, are not passive in relationship

to our environment, but are challenged to initiate novelty to match the novelties we experience. Our spiritual and ethical vocation is to choose wisely, nurturing beauty and wholeness of experience and honoring creativity, for the well-being of our communities and the planet.

4) *Gentle Providence.* As Paul asserted at the Athenian marketplace of ideas, God is the reality in whom we live and move and have our being. God moves in and through all things, providing visions of possibility and the energy to embody them. God's gentle providence is available in every situation, providing the inspiration for dreams, visions, and creative responsiveness, and revealing a way where forward when we perceive no path ahead. Every encounter has a deeper meaning, and can contribute to our own spiritual growth and the growth and well-being of others. In a world of adventure, God is the Holy Adventure whose love inspires compassion and creativity.

5) *Universal Empathy.* Process theology asserts that God is the most moved mover. In contrast to those who see perfection as changeless, process theology sees God as the fellow sufferer who understands and the joyful companion who celebrates. God experiences the world, both the inner and outer dimensions of life, and God's experience of the world inspires God's own Gentle Providence. God hears our prayers and responds with sighs too deep for words. Ever-present and embodied in our world of change, God feels our every sorrow and delights in our every achievement. Nearer than our next breath, God inspires us to commit ourselves to empathetic companionship with those around us, both human and non-human. In hearing the cries of the poor, we hear God's voice, and receive guidance in our vocation to be God's companions in healing the Earth.

Ministry, in the world described by process theology, is lively, adventurous, appreciative, creative, and empathetic. Ministry is inspired by the One who delighted – and still delights - in lilies, soaring birds, playful children, adult creativity, and healing energy.

6

Ministry can be enchanting and beautiful. Despite uncertainty and challenge, our ministries can be creative, zestful, and grateful for the wonders of life and adventurous profession toward which God calls us.

7

CHAPTER TWO

MINISTRY AT THE SPEED OF LIGHT

Philosopher Alfred North Whitehead asserts that the higher organisms initiate novelty to match the novelty of the environment. Whitehead's observation describes the cultural and spiritual challenges of the second decade of the twenty-first century. The processes of change are both expanding and escalating, touching virtually every aspect of our lives, including the conduct of ministry and congregational life.

Twenty years ago, I purchased my first cell phone. It was unwieldly and could do only two things – make and receive calls. Today, the cell phone in my pocket is a powerful computer, camera, GPS, recording device, electronic mail platform and information gathering system, music and video library, and data storage device that responds to verbal requests, and every so often, I even use it to make and receive phone calls or text messages. In a few minutes, I will lay down my laptop and check the morning headlines on television, curious as to the nature of the 45th president's latest "tweet," a word virtually non-existent until a decade ago. When I was a child, we had a large black and white big box television that could receive only two television stations, now we receive over five hundred. News stories were often pre-recorded. Now I receive the news from anywhere on the planet in real time, and not just Walter Cronkite on CBS as we did in my childhood, but BBC, Al Jazeera, Telemundo, and news over my computer or phone as well as cable television. I wrote my first term papers in cursive long-hand and entered graduate school with a Smith-Corona typewriter that required "white out" to correct any mistakes. I felt like I was on top of the world when I got my first Brother typewriter with correcto-type! Now, I write on two or three different computers, with formatting, spell and grammar check, and a plethora of fonts and other options. All these changes have happened in just four decades.

As a culture and church, we have moved from quiet Mayberry and isolated North America to the multiverse and the worldwide web. Blue laws on Sunday mornings have given way to soccer and baseball, and movie theaters now open at times that were once reserved solely for worship services. We are connected in every way, even in monasteries and retreat centers. Once we could speak of North American religion in terms of Protestant, Catholic, and Jew; now the spiritual smorgasbord includes Buddhists, Hindus, Muslims, Shamans, new agers, pagans and wiccans, and even atheists may claim a "religious preference." There is no monopoly on spirituality, religion, or perspective, as spiritual seekers put together a bricolage of faith traditions with little regard for theological coherence. Although politicians and religious leaders speak of returning to the glory days of the 1950's and a mythical "moral" America, even these leaders tweet their bloviations and post inane updates on Facebook and Instagram. Whether in politics, government, business, or religion, deep down we know that we can't respond to twenty-first century challenges with twentieth-century solutions. Just as the United States must contend with growing international power centers, today's churches and ministers must recognize that they are no longer the only game in town. The rise of the "nones," "dones," and "spiritual but not religious" challenge our sense of calling as well as its understanding of truth, worship, theology, and mission.

Ministers and priests can no longer assume that people know what we are talking about when we use the traditional language of faith, have any sense of scriptural authority, respect for ministry, or sense of the sacred. When visitors come to Christmas Eve services, we can't assume they know the traditional carols or the story of Jesus' birth. Some may even wonder why we're not singing "Rudolf the Red-nosed Raindeer," "Frosty the Snowman," or "A Holly Jolly Christmas" along with "Silent Night."

Years ago, a best seller asked, "Who moved my cheese?" Today, many of us who have been in ministry for decades are faced with a similar question, "Who moved my church?" The mainline has become the sideline. The high-steeple village church at the center of town has become an era piece, a quaint setting for photos or weddings or a picturesque reminder of an earlier, pre-internet era, but seldom do passersby choose to go in even as they enjoy the sound of church bells tolling. Change is unsettling and many yearn for a time when ministry was a "high prestige, low stress" profession, rather than a "low prestige, high stress position." Or, as a recent *Atlantic* article, observed, "Higher Calling, Lower Wages: The Vanishing of the Middle Class Clergy."

One of my favorite images of ministry comes from the film, *A River Runs Through It.* In the film, Reverend Maclean leisurely studies for each week's sermon, poring over poetry, the original Greek and Hebrew, and theological texts. He regularly communes with the Creator while fly fishing and relaxes over an uninterrupted homecooked meal each night. A rare phone call at home usually heralds a pastoral emergency. Even though I have cultivated the habits of prayer, study, morning walks on the beach, and daily outings with my young grandchildren – and I realize my lifestyle is exceptional among pastor-scholars – even a village pastor like myself is on duty twenty-four hours a day, can be reached by my parishioners during a morning walk or at my home study, and even need to respond to e-mails and texts when I am away from home at a conference, talk, or holiday. Not being a Luddite, opposed to technological change, I went on Google as I was writing this morning to ensure I was accurate in my depiction of *A River Runs Through It* and in my definition of the word "Luddite!"

We are always in the best of times and the worst of times, as Charles Dickens notes. I, for one, rejoice that I am alive today rather than the nineteenth or fourth centuries. We can't go back, chronologically, experientially, spiritually, or theologically; nor frankly would we want to. We delight in our technological gadgets and give thanks for pharmaceuticals, pain relievers, and diagnostic and medical procedures that will enhance our quality of life well into retirement. The spiritual and professional challenge is to frame our ministries in terms of creative responses to interdependence, pluralism, rapid-change, polarization, and post-modernism. We need to share our "good news" in a world in which even the atheist is unsure which God he or she needs to deny and in which "truth" has been challenged by intentional "false news" and the growing focus on "designer facts," news outlets that reflect our viewpoints rather than subject us to diverse interpretations of the events of the day. Often, I engage in conversation with ministerial and academic colleagues, motivated by the question, "How do we share the truth as we understand it, when the very idea of truth is in doubt, or when truth is understood as individualistic not communal or global? How do I share the good news of Jesus and his vision of a loving God, when ignorance or perceived irrelevance of that good news is the norm, even among those who regularly attend church?"

We are challenged, as pastors, to be novel in our preaching, leadership, study, communication, and approach to ministry. To shape the world within and beyond the church in relevant ways we must "tell the old, old story" using the language and media of our ever-changing postmodern, pluralistic age. While there is no one way to respond to the dislocations of the present time, I would like to share a few insights for my fellow pilgrims in ministry – and we are all pilgrims these days! – that I have found helpful in my own pastoral adventures. Although I am steeped in the theologies, traditions, and spiritual practices of the church, there are times I sail forth on holy maritime adventures in a spiritually rudderless boat, like my Celtic Christian ancestors, praying that God will guide me, like these ancient Celts, to my place of resurrection, the thin place where my unique spiritual gifts will be most effective in sharing the good news of the way of Jesus in this uncertain cultural and congregational time.

The first thing adventurers must remember is that authentic spirituality is about "location, location, location." As the band REM once sung, "stand in the place where you are" and then turn your head around to find your bearings. All ministry is local and contextual. Though the philosopher Socrates imaginatively explored the universe of experience, his vantage point was the culture and mores of Athens. Jesus brought salvation to the whole Earth, but spent the whole of his life in the precincts of Judea and Samaria. Paul traveled throughout the Mediterranean world, but shared the gospel message to each congregation in terms of its own unique context. At South Congregational Church, where I serve as pastor, we describe ourselves as a "village church with a global perspective." Deeply rooted in the flora and fauna, and ocean tides of Cape Cod, the unique challenges of our aging demographic as well as growing opioid epidemic on the Cape, our ministry focuses on the spiritual lives of baby boomers, while being attentive to the welfare of elders and young families. Still, we also go global with concern for orphans in India, Syrian refugees, and rising sea levels.

Socrates once counseled "know yourself." In addition, we need to know where we are. Discover the intersection of your own unique experience and gifts as a spiritual leader with the holiness and brokenness of your environment. All places are "thin places," where God's presence is revealed to those who pause long enough to discover it. In the spirit of the North African spiritual teacher who asserted that "the monk is all eye," a good pastor is all sense, observing the obvious as well as hidden currents of pain and joy in her or his community, and grounding these observations in the Gentle Providence of God, moving quietly and anonymously, though occasionally dramatically, through all things.

Second, pastoring in an interdependent and rapidly-changing world requires the recovery of the rabbinical spirit. Like Pastor Maclean from "A River Runs Through It," pastors need to see study as a legitimate and necessary form of spirituality. While we may no longer be "renaissance persons," adept in many scholarly, sociological, and scientific fields, we need to be motivated by a curiosity about the human condition and the world in which we live. Today, our studies may range much further than cloth bound commentaries and theological tomes to encompass on-line resources, blogs, media, and digital conversations. Still, our calling as theologians of our congregations challenges us to join the truths of faith with the breaking news and the experiences of persons in our community. The locality of ministry demands big picture thinking – a broad perspective – if we are to rightly connect the biblical story and the wisdom of spiritual guides with the ever-evolving local and planetary community in which we pastor and our congregants live. While pastors may no longer be the best educated persons in our congregations and communities, we must strive to be among the most insightful and large-souled interpreters of the world in which we live by prayerfully gathering information and wisdom and then synthesizing what we discover with God's Good News, incarnate in our communities and the world.

Third, pastors in our changing world must become healers and spirit persons, who seek shamanic convergence of heaven and earth, divinity and humanity. As we will see in the next chapters, today's pastors are the children of mystics, shaman, and healers, who share the divine energy and wisdom they have experienced with communities in which they live. In a world often hell-bent on destruction and promoting death in its many forms, physical, spiritual, relational, and planetary, we must claim our ancient role as life-givers and healers. In contrast to the disenchanted world of consumerism and unrestrained corporate growth, our calling is to re-enchant the world, opening spiritual windows that enable those with whom we pastor to experience God's presence in everyday life and inspiring them to do ordinary things with great love. This involves an openness to the sacred through our own "practicing the presence of God" in our relationships and ministries.

Fourth, open to the holiness of each moment and the interconnectedness of life, our ministries are mission-spirited. Everything we do is aimed at healing the world. Our parish is local, but in an interdependent universe, it must also be global. Jewish mystics assert that when we save a soul, we save the universe, because the healing of the universe requires the healing of each part. Conversely, in bringing wholeness to the planet, we also save the spirits of our human and non-human companions. Look for connection. Embrace the web of life, in which God's center is everywhere and includes everyone. Realize that what happens in your study, a local coffee house where you meet congregants, or the sanctuary is part of greater story of global destruction or wholeness. There is ultimately no "other," even when we must contend with the viewpoints of others in protest or protection of our planet. We are connected, bringing joy or sorrow, awakening to God or dimming the divine vision, by every action we take personally and corporately.

Fifth, be willing to conspire with the laity. George Bernard Shaw once asserted that the professions are conspiracies against the laity by virtue of their erudite, incomprehensible language, and professional distance. While professional boundaries and education are essential to healthy and empowering ministry, we must remember that these boundaries exist to serve and connect with laypersons.

Share good news in ways children as well as adults can understand. Remember the image of God in each person and the power of connection through communication and inspiration. Communicate with love, simplicity, and clarity to open new horizons of spirituality and mission for those with whom you pastor.

While my list is far from exhaustive, and must be worked out in your context of ministry, I believe that process theology inspires pastoral leadership that communicates, joins, inspires, and heals. We are, as pastors, called to reflect the God we follow, interdependent, creative, involved, inspiring, and relevant to the world in which we live. It truly is all in the process, embodied in relationships that heal and transform one moment and one encounter at a time.

CHAPTER THREE
PASTOR AS SHAMAN AND SPIRIT PERSON

Today's minister is the child of the ancient shaman. As pastors, our vocation is to be fallible and limited people who nevertheless encounter the holy and seek to share that experience with others. Despite our obvious imperfections, there is something about God that calls us forward and makes Spirit our ultimate concern as we navigate the details of everyday life and institutional leadership.

In the ancient world, the shaman traveled from the heavens to earth to the underworld and back to the heavens. He or she brought the perspective and energy of Spirit to fallible and hurting humanity. Living in an enchanted world, the shaman saw meaning everywhere and discerned Spirit in all things.

Marcus Borg describes the shaman as a spirit person, open to divinity, aligned with divine power, and called to share pathways of the Spirit with her or his tribe, community, or congregation. Jesus was a spirit person, who encountered God as his deepest reality. Jesus saw divinity in himself and in wayward humankind. Out of his relationship with God, Jesus inspired and energized a group of women and men who transformed the world. Arising from encounter with God's energy of love, Jesus was able focus energy to transform cells as well as souls.

Process theology invites pastors to be agents of creative transformation, whose calling is to re-enchant the world. Awakened to God's gentle providence and creative challenge, today's pastors look for God moments in everyday events and ordinary persons. With the Gospel of Thomas, process theology invites pastors as spirit persons to "cleave the wood" and discover God's presence (77). In like manner, as children of God's light, their calling is to experience God's light flowing through them in such a way that they affirm with Jesus "I am the light of the world" and challenge their congregants and seekers with the affirmation "you are the light of the world" (Matthew 5:14).

15

G.K Chesterton asserted that angels can fly because they take themselves lightly. The shaman faced death and gained new insights, one of which was the tragic comedy of life. Shamans were often clowns and tricksters, and in his own way, Jesus was a playful spiritual leader. He enjoyed irony, humorous parables, and delighted in playing with children. Indeed, Jesus proclaimed that you must be like a child, open to the glorious and everlasting now, to experience divinity. The spiritual quest is so serious at times that playfulness is a necessity. Religions that lack humor are prone to idolatry. Just look at the humorless visages of Muslim and Christian fundamentalists, whose inflexible doctrinal seriousness leads to ostracism, denunciation, polarization, and violence against the heretic and infidel. Humor pokes fun at human pretense and pride and the small hypocrisies and ironies that characterize the habits of saints as well as sinners.

The shaman dances and clowns her or his way toward divinity. It is not accidental that one image of the Trinity is a divine dance involving the three "persons" of the divine. In dancing, we are open to novelty. We begin with tradition and move forward lured by energetic possibilities. Dancing and movement create lively and flexible sacred spaces that surround the dancer wherever he or she goes. Surely, this is at the heart of the Celtic spiritual practice of *caim* or "encircling" in which the pilgrim draws a circle around her or himself as her or she rotates in a clockwise fashion. Wherever you go, the dancing circle announces that you are surrounded by God's love. As another ancient affirmation proclaims, "God is circle whose center is everywhere and whose circumference is nowhere."

Shamanic and spirit-filled ministry experiences God in all things and all things in God. The re-enchanted world of process theology inspires pastors to make sanctuaries and church buildings sacred places and then remind seekers and congregants that their homes, workplaces, schools, and recreational spots are equally sacred. Spirit-filled process-relational ministry expands the sacred circle to embrace non-humans as well as humans and death as well as life. As St. Francis noted, the birds of the air and the animals of the forest share God's wisdom with us. Jesus proclaimed God's love for lilies and birds as well as human beings. God's resurrection spirit enables us to walk through the valley of the shadow of death and discover a way where there is no way, and possibilities where others see only dead ends.

The shamanic and spirit-filled aspects of ministry go far beyond the church. The pastor as shaman lights spiritual fires in her or his congregation and then provides practices that nurture body, mind, and spirit. Beyond that, the pastor as spirit person widens the church's mission to become a spiritual haven for seekers. Process theology's affirmation of God's presence in human and non-human life, and seasons of the Earth, enables the church to respond to the pastoral and spiritual needs of spiritual pilgrims as well as join in solidarity with persons of other faith traditions, including pagans, wiccans, and indigenous peoples. Process theology's affirmation that God is a beauty seeker opens the door for common mission aimed at healing the planet and inspires a church that is both heavenly minded and earthly good.

Open to the deeper movements of God's gentle providence, "the sighs too deep for words," described in Romans 8:26, the pastor, like the ancient shaman, re-enchants the world and brings forth beauty out of ugliness and healing out of chaos and disease and shares in God's re-enchanting of the world.

CHAPTER FOUR
PREACHING FOR PILGRIMS AND SEEKERS

St. Francis of Assisi once counseled "Do all you can to preach the gospel, and if necessary use words." Spiritual growth involves the interplay of sound and silence, and speaking and listening. Process theology asserts that God is constantly addressing humankind through possibilities, intuitions, and encounters. God's "whispered word," as process theologian Marjorie Suchocki affirms, comes initially in "sighs too deep for words." We bring God's omnipresent and oft-hidden word to consciousness through intentional practices, ranging from prayer and meditation to worship and preaching.

Process theology affirms that spirit-centered preaching is a holy enterprise, involving the pastor and congregation as whole persons. Not just intellectual or cerebral, holistic preaching awakens us to God's word and wisdom revealed in the five senses as well as the mysterious unseen realities that inspire and undergird our lives. German mystic Meister Eckhardt proclaimed that all things are words of God. The preached word opens us to divine wisdom, broadly revealed in our own lives, in the non-human world of flora, fauna, air, land, and sea, in quotidian activities of domestic life, cultural creativity, and political decision-making.

Despite the importance of preaching as a search light, illuminating God's healing and liberating presence in the world, the practice of preaching is in upheaval. In a world of multi-sensory entertainment, multi-tasking, sound-byte theologies, and false news, homiletic talking heads seem irrelevant and fifteen to twenty minute Sunday morning spiels excruciating to many youths as well as their parents. Moreover, in a world in which pluralism is countered by designer news and laser-focused cultural and political siloes that create and justify our opinions, alternative and imaginative visions, essential to the preacher's task, intrude on the desire to exclude intellectual and political dissonance and critical thinking.

There is a temptation among preachers not to make waves and simply focus on "feel good" messages that justify our pre-existing prejudices and superficial shibboleths to comfort the agitated, while carefully avoiding agitation of the comfortable. Postmodernism and pluralism appear, at first glance, to render preaching an outmoded enterprise, just one voice and a tentative one at best, in a world in which relativity and uncritical diversity rule. In contrast to such evaluations, I believe that preaching is now more important than ever. Despite the relativity of the myriad viewpoints available at the click of a mouse or a tap of a phone, preaching enables us to discover creative and life-supporting pathways through the maze of pluralism as well as healthy, "relative" truths, to combat "alternate facts," promoted by self-interested and power hungry politicians, corporations, and religious leaders. We can carefully and prayerfully articulate the way of God, present a vision of "Jesus' Abba," as John Cobb avers, and provide practical guidance for the healing and transformation of persons and communities.

Preachers must recognize the essential relativity of the preached word. We cannot claim an absolute perspective, but we can affirm what we have seen and heard as we mediate God's wisdom to our respective communities. We can embrace the promises of postmodernism – constellating around the emphasis on experience, multiple perspectives, and suspicion of uncritical absolutes – as the materials for heart-felt, whole person, and relational preaching, that recognizes its limitations, but points toward encounters with the divine reality in whose dynamic presence we live, move, and have our being. Preaching reveals the holiness of the moment and inspires us to claim our vocation as partners in healing the world.

Preaching is, first, invitational and illuminating. We do not address a godless world, but a community that is chockful of divine revelation. The whole earth is filled with God's glory, as discovers unexpectedly, in the Jerusalem temple. In sharing good news, we invite our congregations to experience good news in their own lives. We invite congregants to listen to their lives in all their mystery and ambiguity, and to trust that a deeper voice, a Gentle Providence, is moving through the interstices of everyday experience.

Second, preaching presents provocative possibilities emerging from a congregation's personal, cultural, social, and political location. "Behold, God is doing a new thing," and so should our sermons. God encounters us with possibilities appropriate to every situation, both individual and corporate. God does not coerce but invites. God does not unilaterally demand, but honors our own freedom and creativity. Provocative possibilities serve as invitations to explore the far horizons of our experience and sojourn toward God's visions of Shalom, healing, wholeness, and justice.

Third, preaching awakens us to the immanent and ambient presence of God. Inspired by his dream of a ladder of angels, Jacob exclaims, "God was in this place and I did not know it." Preaching challenges us to affirm, "God is in this place, and now I know it." Preaching invites the congregation into the deep mystery, quietly moving in their lives. Illuminating and challenging, preaching also provides space for listeners to share in the preacher's own silent reflections and discover God's still small voice in their own silent places.

Fourth, preaching invites us to think big, theologically and experientially. Theologian Bernard Loomer saw size or stature as a primarily spiritual reality. Good preaching invites us to broaden our experiences, to become "fat souls," in the words of Patricia Adams Farmer, who embrace the diversity and pluralism of life. Too many theologies lack stature: they are small in spirit, excluding more of reality than including, and damning rather than embracing. Such theologies limit revelation to a book or a room, to like-minded persons, and miss the ever-changing kaleidoscope of divine revelation. Holistic preaching takes out of our silos and into the world, inviting us to experience others' perspectives as well as our own. Truth is broadcast every moment and even those whose beliefs we challenge have been touched by God.

Fifth, although "location, location, location" is central to ministry, preaching challenges us to move from self-interest to world loyalty. As John Wesley asserted, the world is my parish. Accordingly, every sermon must go global as well as local. Each moment emerges from and shapes the universe beyond itself. Accordingly, every sermon has a missional perspective, aimed at transforming the listener, and preacher, and then aiming them toward claiming their vocation as God's companions in healing the world.

Sixth, preaching is profoundly practical in nature in its integration of vision, promise, and practice. Preaching presents a vision, a way of looking at the world in terms of God's Gentle Providence, the holiness of each person and every encounter, and dynamic interconnectedness of life. Theologically-grounded preaching promises that the preached word about the lively God whom we follow, can be experienced in life-transforming ways. Word and wisdom can be embodied in the daily adventures of domestic, relational, and political life. God is dynamically moving in our lives and we can experience and be transformed by our experiences of divinity.

Finally, good preaching, especially when connected with inspirational adult and children's faith formation, provides spiritual practices that enable us to experience the holiness of everyday and our calling as God's world-healing partners. Preaching inspires regular commitments to spiritual formation practices, appropriate to our personal and cultural context, personality type, and places of growth. The practice of preaching is, from a process perspective, holistic in nature, and contributes to preacher's own spiritual growth. Deep and inspirational preaching, connecting the dots from the personal to the planetary, emerges when pastors take seriously their own spiritual practices and see preaching as an inspiration to study, reflection, and prayer. Preaching involves the inner and outer journeys of faith. The preacher begins in solitary reflection on the interface of scripture, theology, and contemporary experience. The preacher prayerfully consults the wisdom of other spiritual pilgrims by poring over commentaries and texts in theology and spiritual formation. In the stillness of the study, the preacher opens to the maelstrom of cultural and political life, looking for signs of God's presence and challenge in the newspaper, on-line, or in network and cable news. In these private moments, the preacher begins to make connections between God's word and wisdom and the world of her or his congregants. Every aspect of the process of preaching is inspired by God, whether in the solitude of study or the publicity of the preached world. God is here, nudging, illuminating, challenging, comforting, and inspiring the preacher every step of the way.

Reflections on preaching challenge us to briefly consider the interdependence of preaching and worship as revealing in partnership the dynamic and vital presence of God. Worship is public, though it is often planned in private. Location and setting are everything in life-changing worship. Worship emerges from a community's style and ethos, but is also reflective of the pluralism of our time. I often speak of my vision of the church I pastor as a "village church with a global perspective." The "village" pertains to location and tradition, to the gathered community and its 220-year history. Our village reflects our unique personality and gifts. Yet, our village is not bound by our traditions, histories, or current possibilities. The world permeates the village, shaping it indirectly and directly, inspiring us to embrace novel and global perspectives in music and in the language of prayer and worship. Vital and lively worship takes many forms, and forms embrace silence and speech, listening and singing, tradition and novelty, local and global, personal and political, piety and planetary consciousness. The constant emphasis in worship is our alignment with God's aim at beauty and our commitment to do something beautiful for God in the holiness of worship and the wholeness of compassionate caring action.

CHAPTER FIVE
HEALING PRESENCE

Process theologians assert that the aim of the universe is toward the production of beauty, whether in the evolution of galaxies and planets, civil and congregational life, the nurture of children, or spiritual growth. Life, the philosopher Whitehead asserts, begins with the dream of youth, full of possibility and adventure, and finds fulfillment in "tragic beauty," the reality that our lives, at best, are a creative synthesis of affirmation and negation, health and illness, adventure and routine, wonder and pain, and freedom and limitation. Dreams are dashed and hopes decimated by the realities of sickness, family dysfunction, and social injustice. The contrasting public proclamations, "Black lives matter" and "Blue lives matter," point to the reality of violence, injustice, and unnecessary pain, which tragically characterize the daily lives of children, young adults, and public servants.

Life is beautiful. Yet the beauty is too often marred by ugliness in the body politic, civil discourse, intimate relationships, and family life. Beyond the pain brought on by oppression, injustice, violence, and trauma, is the inevitable reality of what Judith Viorst describes as life's "necessary losses." Spirituality, as Episcopalian spiritual guide Alan Jones avers, deals with the "unfixables," that is, what must be endured even in a good life – aging, sickness, and death. These unfixable elements of life can destroy us or they can inspire the spiritual quest that gives birth to a religious movement, whether in Judea or in India, where Jesus and Buddha observed the brokenness of life and sought in response to bring healing and beauty to suffering humanity.

Ministry is profoundly shaped by the realities of death and debilitation as well as grief and alienation. Grounded in process theology, pastors recognize that healing involves body, mind, spirit, and relationships. Healing is a process, and not a static state, guided by God's vision of truth, vision, and wholeness.

Healing is at the heart of pastoral ministry. Healing is often confused with the spectacular theatrics and amazing powers, characteristic of televangelists and faith healings. With an apparent success rate of 100%, such healing ministries suggest that healing is primarily an individual and physical issue, having virtually nothing to do with social and economic structures, jurisprudence, and families of origin. Moreover, these apparently spectacular cures are attributed divine supernatural acts, working through the recipient's deep faith, powerful prayer, or generous financial support. From the perspective of these flamboyant healers, God appears to suspend the laws of nature, providing miraculous cures where physicians have given up hope. Those who are not cured cry out, "Why, O God, have you forsaken me?"

While dramatic healings do occur and many "healers" are authentic and selfless, process theology views healing from another perspective – naturalistic, whole person, often gradual, and social and political in nature. Healing moments, transforming cells and souls, involve a dynamic and synergetic partnership of divinity and humanity in the context of the communities in which we live. God's aim at healing and wholeness goes far beyond the revival tent or television program. God seeks to the well-being of all creation, human and non-human alike.

The quest for healing, like the growing interest in spirituality, has increased, rather than decreased, with the rise of technological medicine. Focus on the body as the primary locus of Western medical healing has reminded physician and layperson alike that wholeness involves our spiritual lives, relationships, social context, and vision of God as well as surgery, pharmaceuticals, chemotherapy, and radiation.

As children of the shaman and spirit person, today's ministers carry the healing mantle of their predecessors, whose mission was to promote the energies of life in the context of sickness and death and to ferry the dying to the next stages of their adventure while assuring the community of the eternal verities of life and love. Christian ministers are also the spiritual children of the healer Jesus. The way of Jesus is the path of healing, whether individual, communal, or planetary in nature. Jesus' mission aimed at transforming spirits as well as bodies in the context of a politically oppressive environment in which the sick were often stigmatized and ostracized. Jesus' twin mission statements focus his ministry and ours on healing and wholeness, personal and social, as a reflection of God's vision of Shalom, peace, wholeness, and beauty at every level of life. Reading from the prophet Isaiah, Jesus described his ministry as the fulfillment of the prophet's dream:

> *The Spirit of the Lord is upon me,*
> *because he has anointed me*
> *to bring good news to the poor.*
> *He has sent me to proclaim release to the captives*
> *and recovery of sight to the blind,*
> *to let the oppressed go free,*
> > *to proclaim the year of the Lord's favor.*
> > (Luke 4:18-19)

In similar fashion, Jesus describes his vocation as a quest for personal and social fulfillment: "I came that they may have life, and have it abundantly." (John 10:10) In line with Jesus' promise that his followers can do "greater things" (John 14:12), process theology affirms that the energy of love activated in Jesus' healing ministry is present in our world today. We can transform bodies, minds, spirits, and social institutions by our acts of compassion, healing touch, and prayerful protest.

Process theology asserts that healing ministry is both local and global. Pastors and congregations are challenged to heal the sick through prayer, touch, comfort, and complementary healing practices, such as reiki healing touch, anointing, and meditation. Led by today's shamanic pastors, the church is challenged to be a laboratory for divine healing, joining high tech medicine with high touch prayer. Pastors as spiritual leaders have the spiritual vocation of providing pathways to prevention by encouraging spiritual practices, dynamic movement, healthy diet, positive thinking, and healthy relationships. Process theology also recognizes the relational and sociopolitical nature of healing and wholeness. Health and well-being depend on healthy communities, characterized by accessibility to health care, healthy environments, economic justice, educational opportunity, and planetary well-being. As spiritual leaders, pastors are called to make prophetic healing central to their ministries.

In today's divisive cultural context, where disagreement often leads to division, and the culture wars often degenerate into hate speech or acts of violence, pastors need to see prophetic healing as essential to congregational and social transformation. Process theology affirms the universality of experience, value, and inspiration. Every person is touched by God and reveals divinity. While diversity is the norm in human and non-human experience, and each creature is unique in its perspective on the universe, we are also joined by the dynamic and intricate web of life and the ubiquitous unifying energy and vision of God. God aims at beauty of experience in the ongoing evolution of the universe and in the growth of persons and institutions, whose quality of experience shapes our planet for good or ill.

In contrast to the graceless "political correctness" of left and right alike, process theology challenges us to see God's presence beneath contrasting positions. Graceful relatedness does not demand agreement, narrowly-defined inclusive language, or shared viewpoints to affirm our common identity as reflections of God's wise and loving experience. God's gentle providence is at work within all of God's often disagreeable, divisive, and distressing disguises, seeking wholeness in every situation. This is our inspiration to place our hope for prophetic healing ahead of our own individual personal and political agendas.

Prophetic healers are persons of stature, who connect personal healing with planetary healing. Recognizing the graceful interdependence of life, upon which all humankind depends, they work for structures of healing and wholeness in families, congregations, communities, and nations. They balance the need for individual and national healing with world loyalty. Far from passive in responding the negative machinations of the powers and principalities, the economic and political institutions that shape our overall personal and planetary healers, prophetic healers "picket and pray," challenging injustice and marginalization and any social or political behavior that stands in the way of God's vision of Shalom, beauty and wholeness. Recognizing their own privilege, prophetic healers affirm what Martin Luther King describes as the intricate fabric of relatedness. According to King, whose doctoral dissertation focused on process theologian Henry Nelson Weiman:

> *In a real sense all life is inter-related. All*
> *men are caught in an inescapable network of*
> *mutuality, tied in a single garment of destiny.*
> *Whatever affects one directly, affects all indirect-*
> *ly. I can never be what I ought to be until you*
> *are what you ought to be, and you can never be*
> *what you ought to be until I am what I ought to*
> *be... This is the inter-related structure of reality.*

Our quest for beauty and wholeness must itself be beautiful. Means and ends, practices and goals cannot be separated. If our religious and political involvement is alienating or demeaning in nature, the results will ultimately marginalize, abuse, and diminish those whom we disagree. Prophetic healers challenge institutional injustice guided by a vision of wholeness and unity for all creation. Everything is connected: we pray for the healing of cells and souls; we present alternative visions of humankind and institutional practice to cure the injustices that abound; and we see the healing of planet as embracing plankton and persons with whom we most disagree. A politics of love often seems weak, just as God defined by relationship and love seems less powerful than unilateral and coercive visions of God. Process theology affirms that God's relational love and our own will outlast racism, sexism, speciesism, and jingoism. Although the future is open and is, in good measure, determined by our actions, locally and globally, God's vision persists, inspiring an adventure of healing images and expanding the circle of justice and wholeness. We can with Martin Luther King and Barack Obama trust God's all-encompassing aim, expressed by Unitarian spiritual leader Theodore Parker in terms of the moral arc of history:

> *We cannot understand the moral Universe.*
> *The arc is a long one, and our eyes reach but a*
> *little way; we cannot calculate the curve and*

complete the figure by the experience of sight; but
we can divine it by conscience, and we surely
know that it bends toward justice. Justice will
not fail, though wickedness appears strong, and
has on its side the armies and thrones of power,
the riches and the glory of the world, and though
poor men crouch down in despair. Justice will
not fail and perish out from the world of men,
nor will what is really wrong and contrary to
God's real law of justice continually endure.

Recognizing our own limitations and fallibility as well as the innate holiness of those with whom we contend, we will follow our better, healing angels, and claim our role as God's companions in healing the earth, from the cellular to the planetary.

CHAPTER SIX
VISIONS WITHOUT GUARANTEES: TRANSFORMING SPIRITUAL LEADERSHIP

I regularly remind my Cape Cod congregation that I have a vision but not an agenda. I affirm the biblical affirmation, "without a vision, the people perish" (Proverbs 29:18). As a spiritual leader, I need to be visionary. I need to have my eyes on horizons of possibility, but I also need to be flexible in joining these possibilities with concrete congregational settings.

One of my favorite biblical stories involves the journey of the magi (Matthew 2:1-12). This story inspires me, first, because it portrays God's revelation as global, ranging far beyond the Jewish people. It affirms the ubiquity of truth and revelation, captured in the phrase, "wherever truth or healing are present, God is its source." But, just as important to me is the wise ones' response to Herod. Warned of dangers to the Christ child, they return home by another road. They had a vision, a road map home, but they were willing to revise it to achieve a greater good. What would have happened if the magi had neglected to follow the divinely-given dream? Would Herod have slaughtered Jesus along with the other young children?

Ministry is grounded in visionary spirituality. The pastor as spiritual leader is challenged, today more than ever, to imagine alternatives to current congregational and cultural life. He or she is inspired to join big visions with concrete limitations to draw forth the gifts of her or his congregation. Grounded in her or his own spiritual practices, the pastor as visionary leader and administrator is committed to imaginative scenarios of faithfulness for her or his congregation. Her or his ability to nurture and share imaginative visions may be a matter of life and death for her or his congregation.

In *The Awakened Heart*, psychiatrist and spiritual guide Gerald May advises spiritual pilgrims to pause, notice, open, yield and accept, and respond. Spiritual leadership is, first, a matter of

29

pausing long enough to notice what is around you, the unique spirit and identity of your congregational or ministerial setting. A North African spiritual teacher described the monk as "all eye." I would expand this description to embrace all the senses, including the occasional mystical, intuitive, and paranormal experiences that undergird everyday consciousness. Leadership grows by seeing and listening, intuiting and praying. God is moving through every moment of life and every person. Accordingly, any moment can usher us into "the holy of holies" and any person, including a colleague, assistant, or challenging sparring partner, can reveal God's vision for your ministry and pastoral context. All things are words of God, wrote Meister Eckhart. All encounters reveal God's vision, in greater or lesser degrees, process theology.

Today's spiritual leaders must, as Whitehead counsels, initiate novelty to match the novelty of our environment. Today, most leaders must confess that there's almost too much novelty to deal with these days. Flexibility, adaptability, creativity, and imagination are at the center of process-relational leadership, not only because the times demand agile leadership, but also because such virtues reflect God's character and presence in the world. God is constantly presenting us with new possibilities, appropriate to our context. Faithfulness to God means looking forward to the next adventure, whether it be in a brief ministerial encounter, an unexpected phone call or building crisis, or long-range congregational visioning. Although there are times in which pastors need to cultivate sabbath rest for themselves and their communities, pastors must also reach out to embrace novel possibilities and even anticipate novelties that are still on the cultural or religious horizons. This is the spirit of what Walter Brueggemann describes as the "prophetic imagination," the envisagement of alternative possibilities to the current institutional, political, and cultural environment.

Process-relational thought experiences God moving in all things, and this inspires reverence for life, most particularly those with whom we live and work. Office staff and congregational board members reflect God's presence as their deepest reality, inspiring spiritual leaders and intuitive administrators to listen for God's voice in their voices and God's dream in their hopes. Leadership by affirmation and gratitude notices the holiness of our colleagues and prayerfully nurtures experiences of the divine, albeit subtle, in the daily tasks of congregational life, answering the phone, typing the bulletin, or going over church finances. Everything we do is holy and reflects, in a greater or lesser extent, God's visionary presence. Healthy spiritual and congregational leaders say "thank you" and notice "excellence" whenever it occurs, thus creating a graceful, affirmative environment for everyone in the congregation.

Following the counsel to be "all sense," process-relational spiritual and congregational leaders are detectives of the spirit, constantly looking around and asking themselves, "What am I missing? Whose voices are unheard? What persons' wisdom am I neglecting or avoiding?" Even a stopped clock is right twice a day, and even our critics are touched by God's wisdom and may be able to provide helpful counsel in certain situations. In a world filled God's glory and inspiration, we are challenged to find collaborators and wise counselors in the most unexpected persons and places.

Process relational spiritual leadership is affirmative, appreciative, imaginative, and celebrative. On the one hand, God is the fellow sufferer who understands. God feels the pain of the world and responds with healing, and the hope of tragic beauty. On the other hand, God delights in children's laughter, shimmering seas, lovely vistas, humorous asides, and loving companions. The church needs to awaken to divine joy. In the beauty of holiness, we can celebrate that God is still speaking and that God's makes a way even for small and struggling congregations where we perceive no way.

Spiritual leadership and administration, are holy tasks, intending to expand God's influence in the world and awaken people to God's gentle providence and amazing grace. Within the process, our visions and agendas are relativized and then expanded to move us from individual to communal and parochial to planetary affirmation and healing.

Chapter Seven

LIFE IS BEAUTIFUL

The aim of the universe is at the production of beauty, so says philosopher Alfred North Whitehead. God is beautiful and God is constantly seeking beauty in the non-human and human world. Beauty of experience involves the interplay of intensity and calm, contrast and variety, and harmony and innovation. Beauty is ever-evolving and God's vision in the slow process of evolution is toward the emergence of creatures able to experience and embody beauty. In the interplay of God and the world, God inspires and energizes the quest for beauty and creativity. All creation incarnates, to greater or lesser degree, God's vision as its gift to its creator. God is, as Whitehead says, the poet of the world, who leads by the divine vision of goodness, beauty, and love.

Sadly, the beauty of holiness and wholeness has often been neglected in the life of the church and professional ministry. We have focused on budgets, social involvement, and doctrinal fidelity to the exclusion of the simple heartfelt beauty of holiness. We have forgotten that our calling, as theologian Patricia Adams Farmer asserts, is to embrace a beautiful God and then, in the spirit of St. Teresa of Calcutta, do something beautiful for God.

Can ministry be beautiful? Can pastors be artists and poets? Can those who follow the way of Jesus add to the beauty of everyday life and the ongoing beauty of the universe? Can our ministries be artistic adventures, bringing beauty to each ministerial encounter?

I believe that the promotion of beauty of experience is one of primary callings of the church, which occurs not only in lively, inspiring, and well-crafted worship services but in everyday pastoral encounters. We are always on holy ground, and we can be angels – messengers of God and divine artists – to one another by doing ordinary things, as Therese of Lisieux counsels, with great love.

The call to beauty can come in unexpected ways. Recently, as I was flying from Boston to Washington DC, I struck up a brief conversation with my seat mate, a medical student returning to classes in Bolivia. When I encountered her again at the luggage kiosk, she appeared anxious and I inquired, "May I help you?" She responded that she had a small bag on the plane and was worried about making her overseas connection. A stranger with only modest facility in English, she was unsure what to do. I offered to introduce her to an airline representative and then waited with her while they expedited her passage to her next flight. A small encounter, that each of us may eventually forget. But, I know that in reaching out to this anxious pilgrim, I calmed her spirits and added beauty to her experience.

Jewish mystics say that when you save a soul, the universe is saved. Wholeness cannot be achieved until each spirit is reunited with God. I would assert that the universe is saved and healed one encounter at a time. By doing something beautiful for God in very moment, we tip the scale from death to life, chaos to creative transformation, and pain to wholeness.

How can we make our ministries a work of art? How can we bring beauty to our congregational leadership and church life? Process theologians believe that God is the most moved mover. God has a vision, aligns that vision with concrete realities, and then imagines new possibilities in terms of our responses to God's vision. God's beauty seeking visions inspire and challenge us to be beauty seekers ourselves, first, by a life committed to listening for God's presence in our lives, in insights and possibilities, and in the world around us. Every encounter whispers divine guidance to us and when we pause long enough to listen, notice, and respond, we can embody in our own unique way God's ever-changing vision for us and the world. Second, we can intentionally seek to make every encounter an opportunity to bring beauty into the world, whether in the lives of our fellow humans, companion animals, or the institutions that shape our lives.

I believe that church can be beautiful. This involves not only doing ministerial tasks with love and creativity, but bringing beauty intentionally into congregational activities. During my doctoral classes at Wesley Theological Seminary, I have my classes travel down Massachusetts Avenue to St. Nicholas Cathedral (Orthodox Church of America) where we bathe our senses in icons. Icons are windows to the divine. As we look at paintings of the holy family and the saints of the church, we experience the holiness of life and are guided to the deeper holiness of God. Far from being graven images or idols, as some evangelical iconoclasts suggests, icons are pathways to divine beauty. Combining the kataphatic, imagistic spirituality, with apophatic, imageless spirituality, icons enable us to experience divinity, while also recognizing that God is always "more" than we can ever imagine.

Everything in worship can be aimed at beauty. We can delight in global as well as local music, create inspirational paraments and altar cloths, adorn the sanctuary with objects from nature and human artifice, and we share beauty in our sermons and reflections.

As part of our personal and congregational spiritual formation, we can encourage what Patricia Adams Farmer describes as "beauty breaks," times set apart of simply experience the beauty of life, whether in our relationships, bodies, the non-human world, and human artifice. Bathing ourselves in beauty awakens us to experience and treasure beauty everywhere.

Process theology is profoundly incarnational. God is truly in all things. God is the reality in whom we live and move and have our being (Acts 17:28). Awakening to beauty sensitizes us to our personal and corporate destructive behaviors. It asks us to ponder as we look, at our behavior or evaluate congregational and political policies, "Will this add beauty or ugliness to the world? Will this contribute beauty or ugliness to God's experience? Do our actions promote beauty of experience or detract from them in the moment and over the long haul?" A spirituality of beauty inspires beautiful ministries that add to the joy and beauty of our precious planet.

CHAPTER EIGHT

CHURCH WITHOUT WALLS

This brief exposition of the resources of process theology for twenty-first century ministry began with a dream depicting a study without walls, suggesting that pastors and theologians need to tear down the walls that separate their professional lives from the intellectual, cultural, political, and spiritual currents that characterize the world today. We need to let the realities of pluralism, postmodernity, post-Christendom, and planetary and political upheaval flow through our studies and sanctuaries, propelling us into the world with a message of grace, inclusion, healing, and hospitality. According to process theology, God is the most moved mover and the greatest relativist, whose relationship with the world reflects God's own intimate and personal relationality. God's vision of love and quest for beauty is unending, but the shape that vision is personal and contextual.

At the congregation I pastor, we have become committed to ministry without walls through our outdoor ministry on the beach and woodlands near our congregation. We have reveled in the beauty of Nantucket Sound and Craigville Retreat Center. Yet, we are discovering that the Spirit may be calling us to the great outdoors in new and creative ways, as we ponder ministries with homeless adults, youth, and children in nearby Hyannis and initiating outdoor worship services in partnership with other congregations on the village green in the fabled holiday destination of the Kennedy family.

While brick and mortar, sanctuaries and steeples, are sacred spaces where we experience God's vision and guidance, the whole earth is full of God's glory and in need of God's healing touch. Whether pastoral or congregational, ministry takes out onto the streets and beaches and into the coffee houses and homeless shelters to share the good news of God's love for all creation. Moreover, a church without walls opens us to dialogue with persons of other faith traditions, agnostics and seekers, as well as those who have been politically and economically marginalized due to race, gender, or sexuality.

Martin Luther King once referred to Sunday morning as the most segregated hour in America. Today, we have expanded King's critique to recognize that millions of Americans live in political and ideological silos, listening only to the political and religious voices that confirm their beliefs and distrusting any dissonant voices, and including those of prophets, encouraging more global, welcoming, and critical viewpoints. The focus on the relativity of truth and experience as well as pluralistic perspectives characteristic of postmodernity has been a reactive catalyst for millions of Americans to absolutize their own narrow perspectives and deny the validity of any perspective beyond their own, most especially when their own perspective is shown to be lacking factual evidence. Even within the church, ardent believers absolutize limited viewpoints and implicitly deny more global understandings of divine revelation and inspiration. Open-spirited Christians must go beyond such thinking, despite our own temptation to intellectually marginalize and demean those with whom we disagree.

Affirmation of God's ubiquitous presence requires us to look for glimpses of divinity where we think they are least likely to be found – in opioid addicts and homeless veterans, terrorist cells, and advocates of white supremacy or consumers of Breitbart news. Even here we must open to God's still small voice, whispering to us in those voices we least wish to hear. We need to be persons of stature, able to embrace diverse and contrasting persons and perspectives, without losing our spiritual center. Our commitment to Christ's path as pastors and spiritual leaders is a call to spiritual expansiveness and not ideological contraction. As spirit persons, our task is to experience the "wideness of God's mercy" and healing power and invite our congregations to become vehicles of God's all embracing, all transforming love.

Here on Cape Cod, where I live, I use our outdoor shower daily between May and October. Although the shower has walls, it is "room without a roof," to quote Pharrell Williams. I am, as Williams' song says, truly happy when I shower outside. On a summer morning, I can observe the seagulls, cardinals, and an occasional osprey flying overhead. On an evening after a day at the beach, I delight in a sky full of stars. I experience wonder at the expansiveness of the heavens as well as the breadth of the sea. Today's church needs to create its own spiritual skylights, joining heaven and earth and global local to share in God's healing and inspiring presence. We need to look up to find perspective and liberation from the isolation of siloed theology, ethnicity, economics, and politics. We need to look around to discover holiness in every encounter and person. Looking upward and outward reminds us that everything we do is mission. Everything we do as pastors and congregations radiates beyond ourselves and can contribute to the healing of the world. We need to look high to glimpse divine vistas of possibility and we need to look far to imagine the horizons of God's adventurous love which call us to care for the children of 2100 as much as the children who race up the church aisles and our backyards today. Finite though we and are congregations are, we need to visualize a boundless love, without walls or roofs, that binds us with all creation. Like the monarch butterflies that inspired the poetic imagery of the butterfly effect, our small actions, like the flapping of wings of a fragile butterfly on a California cliff, can radiate across the planet, sharing in God's vision of a lively, interdependent, and all-embracing quest to heal the world. We can experience God's process shaping and energizing our ministries.

BOOKS TO LIVE BY

Allen, Ronald. *Theology For Preaching: Authority, Truth, and Knowledge of God in a Postmodern Era*. Nashville: Abingdon Press, 1997.

Brock, Rita Nakashima, and Rebecca Parker. *Proverbs of Ashes: Violence, Redemptive Suffering, and the Search for What Saves Us*. Boston: Beacon Press, 2002.

Cobb, John. *Jesus' Abba: The God Who Has Not Failed Us*. Minneapolis: Fortress, 2016/

Coleman, Monica. *Making a Way Out of No Way: A Womanist Theology*, 2008.

Epperly, Bruce. *Becoming Fire: Spiritual Practices for Global Christians*. Vestal, NY: Anamchara Books, 2016,

_____, *Healing Marks: Healing and Spirituality in Mark's Gospel*. Gonzales, FL, 2014.

_____, *The Mystic in You*. Nashville: Upper Room. 2018.

_____, *Praying with Process Theology*. Anoka, MN: River Lane Press, 2017.

_____, *Process Spirituality*. Gonzales, Fl: Energion Publications, 2018.

_____, *Process Theology: Embracing Adventure with God*. Gonzales: FL: Energion Publications, 2014.

_____, *Process Theology: A Guide for the Perplexed*. London: T&T Clark, 2011.

_____, *Tending to the Holy: The Practice of the Presence of God in Ministry*. Herndon, VA, 2009.

Farmer, Patricia Adams. *Embracing a Beautiful God*. Chalice Press, 2003.

_____, *Fat Soul: A Philosophy of Size*. Create Space, 2016.

Keller, Catherine. *On the Mystery: Discerning Divinity in Process*. Minneapolis: Fortress, 2008.

McDaniel, Jay. *Living from the Spirit: Spirituality in an Age of Consumerism*. St. Louis: Chalice, 2000.

Oord, Thomas Jay. *The Uncontrolling God: An Open and Relational Account of Providence*. Downers Grove: IVP, 2015.

Rowlett, Martha. *Weaving Prayer into the Tapestry of Life*. Grand Rapids: West Bow Press, 2013.

Suchocki, Marjorie. *In God's Presence: Theological Reflections on Prayer*. St. Louis: Chalice Press, 1996.

_____, *The Whispered Word: A Theology of Prayer*. St. Louis: Chalice Press, 1999.

Websites that feature themes in process theology:

Jesus, Jazz, and Buddhism (jesusjazzbuddhism.org)

Process and Faith (processandfaith.org)

TOPICAL LINE DRIVES

Straight to the Point in under 44 Pages

All Topical Line Drives volumes are priced at $5.99 print and $2.99 in all ebook formats.

Available

(The titles of planned volumes may change before release.)

Generous Quantity Discounts Available
Dealer Inquiries Welcome
Energion Publications — P.O. Box 841
Gonzalez, FL 32560
Website: http://energionpubs.com
Phone: (850) 525-3916

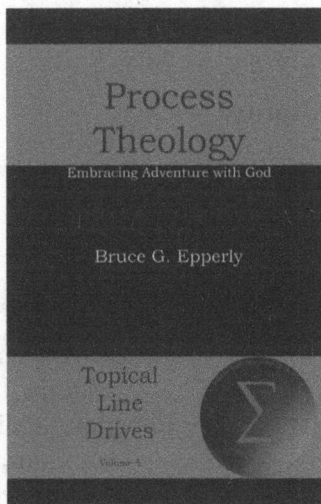

MORE FROM ENERGION PUBLICATIONS

Personal Study

Holy Smoke! Unholy Fire	Bob McKibben	$14.99
The Jesus Paradigm	David Alan Black	$17.99
When People Speak for God	Henry Neufeld	$17.99
The Sacred Journey	Chris Surber	$11.99

Christian Living

Faith in the Public Square	Robert D. Cornwall	$16.99
Crossing the Street	Robert LaRochelle	$16.99
Life in the Spirit	J. Hamilton Weston	$12.99

Bible Study

Inspiration: Hard Questions, Honest Answers	Alden Thompson	$29.99
Colossians & Philemon	Allan R. Bevere	$12.99
Ephesians: A Participatory Study Guide	Robert D. Cornwall	$9.99
Galatians: A Participatory Study Guide	Bruce Epperly	$12.99

Theology

The Politics of Witness	Allan R. Bevere	$9.99
Ultimate Allegiance	Robert D. Cornwall	$9.99
From Here to Eternity	Bruce Epperly	$5.99
The Journey to the Undiscovered Country	William Powell Tuck	$9.99
Philosophy for Believers	Edward W. H. Vick	$14.99

Ministry

Clergy Table Talk	Kent Ira Groff	$9.99
Thrive	Ruth Fletcher	$14.99
Out of the Office: A Theology of Ministry	Bob Cornwall	$9.99
The Space Between	Matt Braddock	$14.99
Tending the Tree of Life	Richard Voelz	$12.99

Generous Quantity Discounts Available
Dealer Inquiries Welcome
Energion Publications — P.O. Box 841
Gonzalez, FL_ 32560
Website: http://energionpubs.com
Phone: (850) 525-3916

www.ingramcontent.com/pod-product-compliance
Lightning Source LLC
Chambersburg PA
CBHW011747020426
42331CB00014B/3314